"People who just go out in sun
on three quarters of the year.

Cover Image: Great Close Scar, left with the track, centre, leading south from the Malham Tarn Field Centre.

STEVE
Sent via Phoebe
with ...
Best Wishes! John V.

INTRODUCTION

Lister Arms, one of the two pubs in Malham Village

I first went to Malham with my school in the 1950s. The effect it had on me was incredible. I still recall drawing a picture of an adder before the trip and being really excited by the promise of seeing snakes during the day. When we got there, it was just a jumble of many wonderful things: the greenness below; the blue above; the little bridge and the two pubs. The magnificent carboniferous limestone everywhere but no snakes as far as I could see.

I have been back to work, play, drink and romance but this year, with little prospect of wider travel, I decided to go every week and see how Malham Moor and its adjacent townships developed over 12 months. Apart from observing the natural environment: creatures, plants and seasonal developments, I wished to keep an eye on my own condition and how this reacted to the external environment.

During the year's progress the themes of Mahler's 3rd symphony: Flowers; Animals; Mankind; Angels & Love came to me time and again. Hopefully the odd comment on each can help me understand and perhaps provide a thought or two for the reader during these next few chapters. Having been each of the 52 weeks and written a diary entry, this is now condensed into 12 monthly chapters. Each week there was no plan; just see what happens but those themes, mentioned above, keep coming back.

A main reference has been the magnificent publication of the self-trained scholar, Arthur Raistrick, whose 'Malham and Malham Moor' has been a constant source of inspiration; titbits appear throughout the following pages. Any quote appears in inverted commas "like this", followed by the page number. Anything else in inverted commas is from my diary with the date. The map below is from Raistrick, page 1 with the 8 townships that border Malham Moor, the subject of this book.

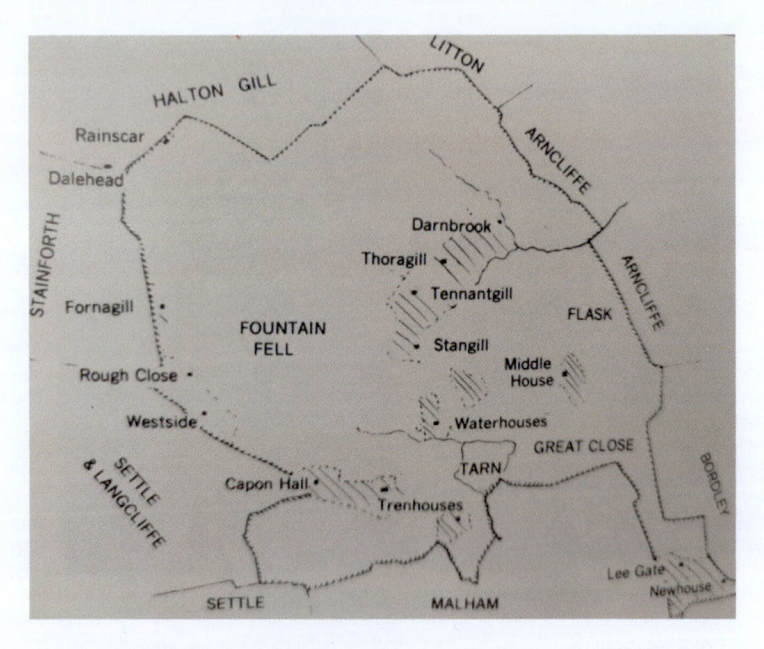

Malham Moor and its 8 surrounding townships: Bordley, Arncliffe, Litton, Halton Gill, Stainforth, Lancliffe, Settle, Malham.

In my diary, reference to the above comes from 21st January: "One thing we mused on later was Raistrick's comment that, unlike most parish boundaries, which were rectangular between river and watershed, 'Malham Moor remains entirely irregular; it is a polygon left between the many out-boundaries of eight parishes'. Raistrick, p. 90. The suggestion is that the lowlanders could not extend to the top of the moor due to 'a new group of settlers' who had squatted high up. 'These Norse people took the wild and neglected outlying fringes and welded them into a new township.'"

Apart from the natural themes, there was the issue which newspapers called 'Covid' and it is interesting to see how people's views changed during the year as they got used to the fact that family and friends often saw this from entirely opposite perspectives. At the beginning of the year, people took different sides on illusionary barricades, calling the other side 'bedwetters' or 'granny killers', depending on which side you stood! As a result, Neil Oliver, came to this conclusion: 'we must learn to deal more kindly with one another'.

JANUARY

"To appreciate the beauty of a snowflake it is necessary to stand out in the cold."   Aristotle.

Indeed, and January is the coldest month of the year on Malham Moor. However, in early January, there are 75 seconds more daylight than the solstice each day while, by the end of the month, there are over 200 seconds more, the same as the 10th of November!!! Those of a pagan nature or oriental approach perhaps, therefore call January the last of the 3 winter months.

Pregnant ewes heading for dropped hay near Street Gate (902657)

The key place in January was Great Close, an area in the SE corner of Malham Moor and a name which has many attachments. There is Great Close hill, whose summit my eldest grandson, Luke, has accompanied me every year of his on this planet; There is Great Close scar, the limestone cliff on the side of the hill; There is Great Close mire and there was Great Close fair with a refreshment house to accommodate "cattle drovers who came down from Scotland and the north" Raistrick, p.99. The picture above shows, not only the ewes, but also Street Gate corner, from where one can head east into Wharfedale, north into Littondale, south into Airedale and west into Ribblesdale!

Above is a typical January day, cold but getting lighter. The 'person of the month' is "the redoubtable John Brown" as I call him in one entry. Another entry says: "a former Ilkley solicitor. We had met by the Wharfe during one of the 'lockdowns' and it turned out we had both been at Leeds Grammar School. Despite JB being my junior, we had the same Masters at school and regaled each other with stories about 'Noddy' Stevens, 'Pug' Fairhurst, 'Beezum' Ramsden and 'Masher' Grange." Jan 12.

John joined me on many of these weekly trips and is interesting in terms of the way relationships develop, from an initial shared interest to regular increments of knowledge and respect for each other. "He retains a quiet decency coupled with a readiness to have a giggle. Being a church chorister, his musical tastes are a little different to mine but we satisfied both tastes when he came to call mixing a Daniel Harding prom of Sibelius's 4th symphony followed by Schubert's Luciano Berio." Jan 12.

What I have come to admire about JB is his incredible eye for beauty. Whether it be a limestone crag or an ancient church or a single isolated thistle, he spots it immediately and waxes lyrical. He is also a passionate learner and expresses great gratitude for information such as when we crossed the watershed of Britain. Similarly, he was most grateful for tips on moving in snow and similar things; almost childlike in his enthusiasm. "John expressed quite movingly how he had been up many times over the years but never really experienced the winter snows and how its beauty was of such a high quality with the ever-changing lightness of the sky." Jan 21.

JB blasting a route round Great Close Hill. Jan 12.

As for 'Covid', being a sceptic, I never accepted what the authorities said and, at the same time, looked at basic Virology & Immunology texts and engaged in the 'debate' about current research conclusions. My first instinct was tough: "people telling me I had to stay 'local' due to some fascist decree from London." Jan 5. However, there were benefits: the restrictions are what caused me to write this book, they also made me study and understand science and research better, they made me value democracy and appreciate the sacrifices my parents had made, and they have made me realise the importance of core values in a person and the need to understand 'the other'.

For now I'll stick to the natural world which seems to just carry on, taking no notice of human interests. My MBA dissertation was based on a 'Group-development model' based on this nature and also on the history of Malham Moor and included a number of dates/sites which participants had to research and visit; Malham Tarn with its Silurian slate base (420 myo), Great Close Scar with its Carboniferous limestone (350 myo) and more recent Mesolithic and Roman evidence. Groups on courses had to provide proof that they had all been together on the summit of the hill below.

From Great Close summit (904667). The picture above epitomises this place for me as it is the moor, not the village, which is Malham. The picture freezes it in its winter coat with the road running left-right from Middle House, a Norse farm, to Street Gate and then down into Malham village. Over to the left are the remains of the Roman camp and in the centre ground is Great Close Mire where Mesolithic flint tools, sometimes 10,000 years old, can be found after heavy rain.

FEBRUARY

"Each at watch for each; Sap within the hillside beech, Not a leaf to see." Michael Field.

Gargrave Bridge, over the Leeds Liverpool canal.

February, the coldest month of the year in Britain, would be considered by most people to be winter, I suspect. Using daylight hours, however, it is the first month of spring, with almost 2 hours daylight being added from its first day to its last. Scottish 'winter' climbers love it as it is also the first of the drier months of the year in Aviemore. Cold & dry are perfect conditions and Malham Moor can be seen as a minituarised version of all of that.

In the picture above there is 'not a leaf to see' and this is something I have only just learnt this year; namely, that December had amazingly green grass while the very earliest spring is as brown and dead as can be. Gargrave is where one turns off the main A65 and crosses the bridge, leaving 7 more miles to Malham village. On a busy weekend this can take a long time, so narrow are the roads and so heavy the traffic and, on show day you're better coming in from the north.

In fact, no faster than the barges on the canal over which the Gargrave bridge spans. The bridge is the most northerly point on the canal which goes south-west to Liverpool and south-east to Leeds! Beyond, "The parkland through Eshton Grange is superb and typical of what one might see in dramas like Downton Abbey. The canal itself was first used in 1774 and was a lifeline for the industrial development of the north, carrying coal and limestone one way and textiles in the other." Feb 5.

Actually, our place of the month and person of the month are the Roman marching camp and Slav, seen below with John Brown on the 22nd of February. Slav, from southern Poland, had adopted myself and JB as his '2 uncles John' and we were lucky to have his company on several of our weekly trips. Apart from being a tremendous personality and great chef, he also has that ability that all Poles seem to share, i.e. he can fix and sort just about anything!

Roman pool (917656): behind Great Close Hill, Fountains Fell & Parson's Pulpit

The Mastiles Roman marching camp is something else and 2 entries are taken from the diary: "All that can be seen now are remains of the 'bank and ditch of earth' under which the soldiers put their leather tents. Here for no more than 3 days, their engineering can still be seen 2,000 years later!" Feb 5. "We alerted each other as we knew our lovely greensward track would soon bisect the corner of the Roman Camp revealing to us the small pool which the ditch-dyke runs through. A great place for the navigator as the track, wall and pool all join together at grid ref 917656." Feb 22. The picture above shows Slav and JB at this very special place. The picture also shows, behind and to the right, Parson's Pulpit, another very special place due chiefly to its impact on me as a young boy, to be detailed later.

Looking at the diary entries, there is not much mention of Covid but several complaints about my own physical state. Looking back, one year later, as I edit these entries, I don't know whether to laugh or cry when I see myself complaining about only doing 5 miles or 12,000 steps on my phone's counter. Never mind, full spring is just round the corner!!! I know I overdo the phrase 'a very special place' but I just don't know what else to say and below is another, where the ancient route eastwards crosses Gordale Beck in fine open country.

Gordale Beck crossing (912655)

I feel only a certain type of person will see something in this. It is almost a moonscape and, rather like a haiku, it has connections to many other things. The stream, flowing towards us, will hurtle in just over a kilometre down Gordale Scar; the hill in the centre, High Stony Bank, leads on to Parson's Pulpit, as remote as anyone would wish on a wild windy winter walk and the path off to the right leads past the Roman Camp and drops then into Kilnsey by its famous overhanging crag.

I finish February's story with an entry about John Brown who had just come through the mist in the picture: "Navigating now in wild country through thick mist, we discussed always knowing exactly where you are so we checked the NNW bearing every 500 steps until we got to where the walls come together. Beyond, looming out of the clag, was Great Close Mire with a good deal of water covering its peaty underlay. This sight had a deep impact on John, and when I told him it had also been a tarn and Mesolithic flints are often turned up in mole hills, it seemed to take him off to a dreamy place. It had a very deep effect on him!" Feb 5.

MARCH

"It was one of those March days when the sun shines hot and the wind blows cold: when it is summer in the light, and winter in the shade". Charles Dickens.

Indeed Mr Dickens, and perhaps why Britain, is so interesting. As the diary says "March is an extraordinary month in the UK. Being the middle month of spring, depending where you are and how the synoptic weather map is aligned, you could get high teens in SW England while minus figures and blizzards rage in NE Scotland. Here in N Yorkshire, it has stayed around C10 with some pleasant sun highlighting the seasonal attractions." Mar 22.

Several thousand magical snowdrops embracing the woods approaching Malham Tarn Field Centre (672897)

At home in Ilkley, a little lower than Malham, I had noticed the green shoots of daffodils on the last day of January and crocuses in full bloom in Feb. Up on the moor things are a little later, snowdrops in March, but charming as the colours begin to leap from every corner. "The mainstream media were worrying that the warm 13 degrees would mean open areas would be overrun with 'Covidiots'." Mar 2. But JB, Slav and I were charmed by the people we met, so keen to get out and lead a normal life.

Two diary entries praise these normal folk: "enjoying nice chats with various people all escaping the 'lockdown'. Interesting for me, a map and compass man, encountering so many people with little idea of exactly where they were. I so admire this; their gut instinct is that they should not be locked up for no reason so they just head out to the remotest place they can find." Mar 2. And from Mar 15th:

"Today there just seemed to be a procession of happy young women, sometimes with a guy in tow but often just out with their pals. These young women, I have often thought, might save the world."

As well as these lovely people, mention must be made of Debs & Lee at the Lister Arms in Malham village: "JB had not met Lee before and thought he must be the manager. As it is, he is 'only a cleaner' but that statement really does need a lot of unpicking. Lee's mother was one of the leaders of a strike at the bed company in Barnoldswick, or 'Barlick' as the locals have it. Having grown up in such a household he has no middle-class angst, accepts his contract, does what he does and always has a smile on his face. One of the most impressive men I have ever encountered." Mar 27.

Cove top (896641) looking towards Watlowes, the dry valley, curving round to the left.

Following our customary £3 meal-deal, we continued up the Watlowes valley which takes you to the Tarn, then curled back the other side of the hills to the right. "During the last ice age, the retreating ice gouged the limestone away from Great Close Hill and exposed Silurian rock below. At about 420 million years old, this is slate and the water is able to sit on its top creating the tarn." Mar 27.

Malham Tarn Field Centre is where we ran courses and, as we passed: "I regaled the boys with tales of driving a mini bus through snow with 14 not very sober financial managers from the former Soviet Union on board." Mar 7. On one such return from the pubs of Settle, while I negotiated the icy roads, the 'merry' students, clutching vodka bottles, decided to sing, but the only song common to the Ukranians, Russians and Kazhaks on board was the national anthem of the former USSR!

Malham Tarn & surrounding meadows with Fountains Fell & Great Close Hill behind. Malham Tarn Field Centre is behind the trees.

Another of the Moor's must visit sites is the bronze age circle, although I guess not many find it. This difficulty makes it a great place for kids to explore; the perfect place to carry a picnic on a bright blustery day perhaps. You can really let the kids' minds wander as they look down the valley, in the picture below, towards Malham village. What kind of beasts would there be? Who might come and attack? How would you protect from the weather? Let their imagination run riot!

The Bronze Age hut circle (894648) can just be made out in the foreground.

The Megalithic Portal says: 'A single hut circle about 8 meters across, tucked away in a gully between Comb Scar & Comb Hill. Protected from the elements by steep slopes to the north, east and west, with an open view looking south towards Malham. The entrance faces east towards the steep slope. This site was found in 1959 & dates from the Bronze Age. Well worth a visit for its location.' I make a point of trying to come and camp here with my grandkids whenever I can as it is a perfect place to introduce them to the mysteries of the natural world!

A quick note on 'camping': well past it now, but we always used to watch for a good spell of high pressure and then set off with as little as possible 'Karriless' not 'Karrimor'. We always took a spacepacker plus flysheet, never the inner tent. This gives half the weight, double the room and an extra benefit, for men particularly! I think it would cope with 6 humans easily and 2 dogs fighting once, according to Mike Spence, doyen of the York Mountaineering club.

Just two more 'must see' sites to mention begin with Gordale Scar (915642), seen in the picture below. Raistrick, p 71 says this: "entering the closed part of the gorge, the sides overhang and there is evidence just before the last Ice Age, Gordale Scar was a great cavern, the roof of which subsequently collapsed. A small fault crosses the Scar between the two waterfalls and forms the cave on the east side of the stream and above the lower fall."

Close to Gordale is Janet's Foss (914633), seen below. It was actually March 15th when we did the fabulous round from Malham village, up the left of the Cove, over the limestone pavement, across the moor, down to Gordale, then past the Foss and return into Malham. For most folk this is quite doable and most enjoyable. When we passed the Foss below, I saw a familiar face which turned out to be Kevin Brown, rugby international, who, along with his wife, Kirsty, dived in the water and had a quick splash around. I later found that many sports teams bring their players for this treatment.

Janet's Foss (914633)

APRIL

"Oh to be in England now that April's there."   Robert Browning.

On April 1st my diary says "So 13 weeks were over, and things had gone fairly well with snow, flowers and then lambs to enjoy. It seemed, with excess deaths finishing last May, the pandemic was done but 'vaccines had been introduced in care homes and many had died.". A quarter of the way through the year I had come to realise that, as a sceptic, it was hard to understand that someone else might have a different opinion. Trying to understand this and why family communication had become so whittled down became a source of much anguish.

Approaching the top of Goredale Scar with Goredale Beck down to the left.

Mahler mentioned 'Flowers, Animals, Mankind, Angels and Love'. I wondered what 'Angels' could mean and such mysteries are rather special because anything which makes you think at a deeper level expands you as a human being. I discovered it as I saw less of some family so went often to look for my 2 youngest granddaughters, Harriet and Rosie. They had not yet had the full experience of 'dark sarcasm in the classroom' as Pink Floyd put it. I read with H, played hide & seek with R and even just watched their songs, dances and antics. Absolute angels, always able to make me fly once more!

Talking of flying, when checking for sand martins, I go through the charming village of Bell Busk and look at the far bank of the incipient River Aire, then head off to the top of the moor to Low Trenhouse farm where swallows and house martins can usually be found, once they have got established. JB and I had the good fortune to see the first sand martins (Riparia Riparia) but could see nothing flitting around up at the farm. We stopped for a few moments just in case and then John shouted "look, up there". No swallows or martins but a lazy old tawny owl (Strix Aluco) fast asleep or so it seemed.

Tawny Owl, Strix Aluco, guards Lower Trenhouse farm (889660).

April 19th diary says: "This has been one of the driest Aprils I can remember." In fact it was perfect walking weather, whatever your physical state, and one such walk deserves a mention. "Drove past Gordale and parked at the end of the track, headed NW crossing Mastiles Lane until we reached the Roman Camp joining 2 previous walks, then we retraced down Mastiles and turned south to the village of Bordley which has a strange feel. No public road leading in or out. Getting back with 12,000 steps under the belt, a good dose of vitamin D and some wonderful, inspiring bird sightings led to a jolly return to the lower Wharfe valley." Apr 13.

Another April walk JB and I had was the 26th when we tried once more to get up Fountains Fell from the south, something we had failed to do twice in earlier snows! The southern trig point in the picture is known as Knowe Fell and is a good place for a view of Pen y-ghent. My comment was this: "JB is moving much better than I but I hung in remembering not to push too much. When we reached the trig point, we not only got a view of Pen y ghent to the west but also the Tarn to the southeast."

Pen y-ghent from Knowe Fell trig point (866687).

Coming off Fountains Fell, my diary says: "We lost the track and found the going tough as a result so cut to the right and looked down to Tennant Gill. We initially did the right thing but then a choice of tracks appeared and I took a bearing which, while initially right, started curling left, left, left such that we hit the road again, adding at least a mile to the journey. A classic mistake – always know exactly where you are, every single minute, especially when not so fit." Apr 26. Sheep tracks can often lead to an 'unwanted dipping' as my old mountain buddy, the Earl of Hawkright used to say!

Navigating is interesting – go in the hills and you'll see someone 'in charge' whereas everyone in a group should know where they are and what they are doing. This is one of the key things we used to 'teach', through experiential learning on our courses up here since the same principal applies at work. A classic I remember was when I followed a group with an older Indian male storming off, map flying about in his hand and 4 younger Asians grimacing behind him. Just after the turn off point, I stopped the group and asked a young Thai lady where they were. She hadn't a clue, the Indian guy apologised, and I still wonder if any of them remember the experience? I do and still get it wrong!

Early April sun setting beyond the Ribble valley above Settle

There are 3 ways to Malham for me: Wharfedale to the east, Malhamdale to the south and Ribblesdale to the west and such was the dryness of this particular April, the setting sun just had to be experienced. I remember a proper photographer saying "it's just another effin sunset" but, for the amateur with only a mobile phone, it's a memory. At the beginning of this month, the quote was from Browning but I almost put in the following from Chaucer: "Aprille with his shoures soote, the droghte of Marche perced to the roote." It's another memory and a classic with scholars telling us 'droghte' means 'drought'. But I know it means 'draft', i.e. wind, as Chaucer was in my class at school and he told me!

MAY

"At last came the golden month of the wild folk-- honey-sweet May." Anonymous.

"The focus was mainly to be bird observation as, with 2 weeks of summer gone, nesting has moved to hatching & fledging for many of the temporary visitors." May 13. This reminder of the different perceptions of the seasons (between humans & creatures) was wonderfully expressed by Ray Mears, the wilderness expert, when he said: 'in early March, mother nature's plans are already well advanced'. So, how much further they must be in May!

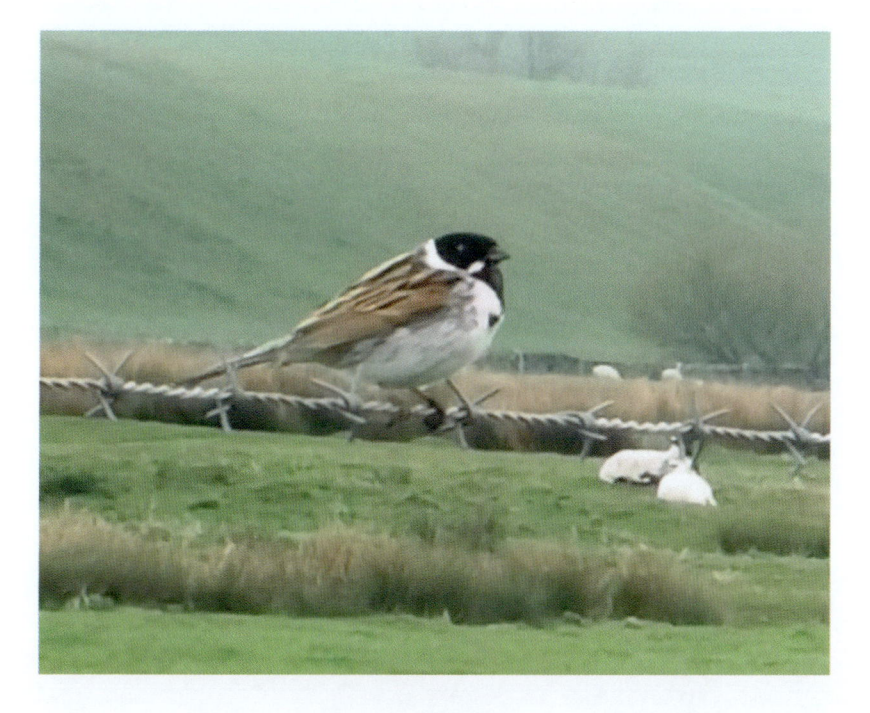

What is it kids???

2 themes, not so far stressed: first, children's education, which had been seriously disrupted this year. From May 19th "Sitting quietly is a wonderful thing as you suddenly see things that a moving person doesn't. Nearing the sand martin site at Bell Busk, something flitted past into the reeds. What could it be? I pulled up and waited." Was it a sparrow? Nah, too much colour. What does the book say kids? 'A streaky brown bird with dark black face, the Reed bunting can be found in wetlands, reedbeds and on farmland across the UK.' Result, Emberiza Schoeniclus.

Pursuing the point, I have already referred to Pink Floyd's song, containing the words 'teacher, leave those kids alone' and the quote above about the wild folk sort of highlights for me the need for the wildness of the individual to be coupled with the discipline of a 'soft culture' where the rules are not imposed but come naturally from common decency, discussion and due respect for the scientific evidence. Some worry that this is going out of the window at the moment.

The second theme refers to 'Mankind' and the diary quote, also Apr 19th says this after reading the farmers' signs saying 'keep out': "However, whether signs saying don't do this and don't do that are the answer, I am not so sure. Most people JB and I engage with are normal working-class people from the big cities and their engagement with their birthright, the beautiful countryside, is fabulous to behold; it is the precise humanity that the rich and powerful have tried to take from us this year!"

Riparia riparia kindly posing at his nest entrance.

Back to the birds; The sand martins had actually been seen in April, but now they were really well established, sharing the egg warming duties. The speed at which they fly means one has no chance of a picture unless they stop like their swallow cousins on a nearby wire. How blessed we were to have the kind soul above stop on the edge of the nest to show us his shape and markings.

As for other animals, namely mammals, we had a brief brush with some of our ancient, extinct cousins when we did a fabulous walk: "starting at Langscar Gate (887648) the going and weather were glorious going west until the track becomes more interesting as it turns south past the famous Victoria, Jubilee & Attermire caves. Here, remains of Hippo, short-nosed Rhino, Hyena and other exotic creatures were found. They lived here during the Pleistocene, hundreds of thousands of years ago." May 1. Great walk, gliding above the townships of Langcliffe and Settle.

Combining the birds with the mammals, my comment from Apr 10th does the job: "Up at Low Trenhouse there was activity also for the first time, with the house martins showing their white rumps to confirm who they were but I had to go back to one field to see a sight I'd never seen before. A ewe with a tyre over her head, rendering her sightless and hungry. Had she been butting her lamb?"

The 'tyred' ewe with her lamb

The May story finishes with a little walk in and out of Stainforth. It is the most northerly of the three Ribblesdale townships which connect to the Moor and a most delightful place. My entry from May 27th says this: "still with elbow pain, I set sail alone determined to get some sun on my face. I went past Catrick Falls and out onto the Henside road and then came back through Winskill. The walk was tough but useful and I chatted to waterfall visitors on a glorious late May day, typical of what we all love; blue sky, high cloud and temperatures well up in the high teens."

Stainforth Church (822673).

In the following week my diary says : "Another funny week started on the 13th when my left arm blew up and I went to the chemist for some cream. "Get yourself straight to minor injuries at Wharfedale" said the guy at the desk. At Wharfedale, I was told "Get yourself straight to A&E at Airedale". I imagined there to be told to get to Calderdale but was sat down and put in a queue. Cellulitis was diagnosed. Having been put on a drip and then had 4 home visits with antibiotic infusions, I was told the diagnosis might be wrong."

I couldn't see a GP but still received continuous messaging offering me both 'Flu' and 'Covid' jabs and it was about this time that my research took me to the Nuremburg Code and the ensuing Helsinki Protocol for medical ethics. Just 2 of the key articles from the latter are relevant here: "The patient's welfare must take precedence over the interests of science and society. (Art 5)"; "Ethical considerations must always take precedence over laws and regulations (Art 9)." I wondered when I read these, how many people were aware and, more to the point, how many would be bothered if they did know??? Perhaps, in another world, these precepts would be on the wall of every hospital ward.

JUNE

"Live in the sunshine. Swim in the sea. Drink in the wild air." Ralph Waldo Emerson.

Interesting June in which I did two trips north to the Highlands. I surprised myself at the beginning of the month by blundering overnight over three Munros, visiting some pals, and then having another late-night sortie on Mount Keen which got my fullest attention, hitting the summit after 11 pm, then dozing in the heather for a couple of hours on the way down. A day's boat ride to Stornaway was the 'rest' in the middle. On the second trip I took a dear Peruvian friend, Ricardo, on a pilgrimage to Iona, dropping him at the Oban ferry and leaving him to it.

My friends further north, we call the Plums and I have certainly never met a more incredible family. Pete, a first-rate chef, always has my goblet shined and Pam, who seems to have a hundred jobs, comes back about 9 and joins a great meal/drink/natter in front of a roaring log fire, whatever the month. 3 kids, Kate, Marc and Iain I love like my own and was so fortunate to meet the boys and Pam in Hong Kong for her 60th. I was also honoured to say a few words when Kate got wed.

Erratic with Ingleborough in the background.

As for Malham Moor, having encountered another erratic above, JB and I went up Fountains Fell from the north-west parish of Halton Gill on June 3rd. "We went up the Pennine Way from Dale Head onto the summit of Fountains Fell. I was reasonably pleased with the ascent on an excellent track and we stopped for our sandwich just before the summit. JB was interested in the coalmine shafts on the top while I heard the mournful cry of my best friend and favourite bird, the golden plover. JB it was who spotted her first but unfortunately, she was not quite amenable enough for a picture".

I think the rest of the month is going to be devoted to, if not one fellah, then one species, falco peregrinus, which even those who are not Latin scholars can probably work out. We had kept dropping by the top of the Cove just to see if there was any sign and it was Friday 18th when I entered this in the diary. "someone told me 4 chicks had hatched and there were 3 females and one male. 2 were just to the right of the nest huddled together while one more was way over to the right."

This got me hypothesising, a problem with retired Research Methods teachers. Was it the size that gave away the gender but, if so, wouldn't the first hatched be bigger? Are the 2 huddlers females and would that mean anything anyway? Is the bird posing for pictures more of a risk-taker and is that evidence of maleness? 2 days earlier we had been to Bempton cliffs which helped. We met researchers, one mapping nests, the other comparing feeding habits of guillemots and razorbills. Those birds are a wonderful way of getting kids into research. I remember my grandson, William, noting the size, colouration and beak shape differences when he was quite young." Jun 18th.

Slav seems to have acquired a particular love of the limestone pavement at the head of the Cove, which is basically where the falcons live. The three musketeers below are also quite interesting, with me in the middle and Slav taking the 'selfie'. JB has come from an Anglican background, Slav from a Roman Catholic one and my mother was a Quaker but I went another way. Humanist I guess but interested in the life of Jesus and enjoying the trips in and out of Dales churches which is JB's forte.

The 3 twitchers on Malham Cove's limestone pavement: Slav, JV & JB.

June 24th it was, however, when we encountered our hero, 'Perry'. The diary takes over here: "Using previous knowledge, we kept to the left when we approached the cliff and there was a single guy with a long lens who informed us there was a young bird lying just below us. Unfortunately, it was so snuggled into the ground, we could not get a picture and I knew that, when we went over to the Cove top, we would be too far for anything good.

Never mind, the day was glorious and refreshing and we had a chat with various people and saw some great displays from the parent birds. Sighting sitting individuals was not easy, however, until one decided to scream at us 'look at me, look at me'. Just to our left and a few grassy ledges down. When we left to get above him the real fun started. Slav climbed down 3 ledges, put his mobile over the cliff and started clicking. "John, my camera's no good; give me yours". As I watched, I thought I would never see the phone or Slav again, but the underneath is what he got!!! Stunning!" Jun 24th.

Falco peregrinus, adult male, I think.

JULY

"Summer will end soon enough, and childhood as well."   George Martin.

Indeed, the 13 weeks with the longest days finish about the 5th August so, to pagans, July is the last summer month although the temperature lag means it is usually the warmest and things tend to be quite slow as you might expect so soon after the summer solstice. In fact, looking at my diary entries, there is so much as though the abundance of high summer had spilt over into my writing. We visited some notable, but less understood, features of the moor, beginning with the calamine chimney.

Slav approaches the chimney (883660), dodging a face mask en route!

Raistrick, p 84 says this: "The New Calamine shaft, 60 feet deep, was sunk in 1806 to reach a complex of veins from which calamine, an ore of zinc, was obtained. The zinc ore ... known and used in calamine lotion was found before 1795 and the mines were flourishing about 1800 to 1930." Referring to ores of copper, Raistrick says "search the heaps and fragments of malachite, brilliant green, and azurite, brilliant blue will be found." The diary makes an observation showing the difference between the unending behaviour of the natural world compared to the fear-induced human one: "We were amazed to find a mask discarded on the path, which surely few ever use, but then delighted to find a pair of skylarks ascending into the clouds above us in full throated song."

We had all felt lethargic and unmotivated but: "The short walk in a strongish breeze did us a power of good! During the wandering we saw the usual collection of beasts including this old bull sitting, lazily chewing the cud, while his consorts actively rip the grass from the field's carpet of green."

Answered the job advert: "no salary, free food, as much sex as you can manage".

Apart from the birds and the mammals, one of the things I really got into studying was thistles. My knowledge soared from about 1% to 5% during the month's study and here was another fabulous way of introducing children to the scientific approach to life, so desperately needed, some would feel, in this age of conflicting information! As Feynman famously said "It doesn't matter how beautiful your theory is, it doesn't matter how smart you are. If it doesn't agree with experiment, it's wrong."

Carduus nutans? Musk thistle, I think.

I hope I have identified the one above correctly as it is by far my favourite due to its minimal shape, fuller colour and more individual nature, if that is not going over the top in an anthropomorphic way. It is also known as the Nodding Thistle and, apparently its fleshy stem is edible and said to be delicious after peeling and boiling. A further internet search revealed that: 'Medicinally, the leaves have been used as a tonic to stimulate liver function and the flowers have been used to reduce fevers and purify the blood.'

Actually, I like all the thistles, the most common being the spear thistle, 'cirsium vulgare' and the scots thistle, 'onopordum acanthium' which I am not sure I can reliably tell apart. I do love the story also which says the Scots chose the thistle as their emblem after the battle of Largs in 1263 when, apparently, a Norwegian invader, creeping towards the sleeping Scots, trod on a thistle and screamed in pain such that the garrison were woken and a defence could be mounted.

Just one more neglected place before finishing with some humans, Highfolds Scar, directly north, above the Tarn. My diary Jul 23rd said this: "Suddenly something wonderful happened – the heat from the previous days had mellowed to 21C, a breeze was up and I was in a place no-one comes, not even the King of Malham Moor. There was a track to the right but the walls to the left, protecting the summit, were bastions so I decided to wait for another day. I knew I'd be up to 10,000 steps so just pottered and enjoyed the air and the stupendous untouched wild meadow flowers. Retracing my steps, just above the tarn, a pair of kestrels came to say hello and perched for a while but left before a decent image could be got."

Before I get to my most special place, let me make reference to people we met on the moor beginning with Zahir: "What an impressive man, a scout leader from Halifax, I could tell by his gait and the fact that he was alone at 9 pm that he was something. 'Salaam a' Laykum' I said and we got chatting. He was doing 20-odd miles which he does regularly. He picked my brain on camping laws and then we parted company. Then 6 lads & a mat came in to view, off to pray on the moor. The Imam mentioned prayers and when I said 'salah' he was most impressed. I have become increasingly conscious of the pleasantness of the much misunderstood Pakistani community in the UK and see the boys following their sisters' lead, cleverly marrying their upbringing and traditional culture with the 'realities' of the modern world." Jul 21.

The lads chase the Imam up the hill.

Humanity came up again when we met some doctors. "JB is so good in these encounters, making connections easily, often with reference to the 'fine old church you have there'. The doctors were still struggling with living in Teesside but enchanted to find the Dales & Moors on their doorstep. It needs stressing - this is what humanity is about, finding a point of contact in everyone you meet." Jul 31. They were met on the way to Parson's Pulpit "the highest of several tops over the 520m contour on the extensive limestone uplands between Malham Tarn and Littondale." Although there are no footpaths to the top, Parson's Pulpit is between two bridleways, the Monk's Road to the north and the Hawkswick - Malham Tarn path to the south.

The diary says this: "I had first come over here with my friend Martin Payne and his school mates, Foster Dufton & Howard McFadyen. We camped near the summit having set off from the Valley of Desolation and it snowed all night on the top with me, 'sans gear', 'sans experience' & 'sans clue'! I remember guys making pancakes & porridge and buying the first ever cheese & onion crisps.

The next morning we had sped, frozen, into Littondale and round into Kettlewell where we had a massive meal, topped off with scones, jam and lashings of tea in front of a roaring fire at the Bluebell Hotel. The price, stored in my head all these years, was six shillings and sixpence, 32 and a half p in modern terms. Absolutely one of the most memorable days of my life!" Feb 22.

AUGUST

"When August days are hot an' dry, I won't sit by an' sigh or die, I'll get my bottle (on the sly) and go ahead, and fish, and lie." Paul Laurence Dunbar.

'Just another sunset'? Well, OK, but such is my love of this hill and its feline shape that I just had to put this in. I've slept on the summit several times, ascended it in all weathers with many lovely people and 40 years ago used to combine it with its two famous neighbours just to see how fit I was. I think 6 hours, 29 minutes was my best time for the 'Yorkshire 3 Peaks'. On this early August day, its reclining shape just seemed to fit with the 'idleness' implied in the quote above.

Sun disappearing somewhere to the north-west over the feline shape of Ingleborough.

Just one more incredible human must be mentioned here, my son-in-law, James, one of the Lumb variety. A lifetime's experience and study have led me to the conclusion that personality is everything and it is something you are clearly born with. In James' case, I don't think I have ever seen a more determined, dogged achiever and that's not to say he doesn't have other qualities. Exceedingly generous, I'll also never forget sitting in a bar in the Lao capital, Vientiane, and receiving a respectful whatsap request for my daughter Elizabeth's hand.

Apart from running the 'Hardsmoor' and completing 110 miles in fewer than 36 hours, he was now running the Dales Way and we were supporting. "First meeting point was the Sportsman Inn in Dentdale meaning we had a drive to Ingleton then a northerly turn, past Ribblehead then northwest down the little road full of railway viaducts which marks Dentdale. From Hawes we went down Langstrothdale, that amazing valley with water appearing to run over limestone before joining its parent river Wharfe at Buckden. From here it is straight down the Wharfe to Ilkley but, to labour the point, in the picture James has completed about 50 miles but still has 30-odd left to do!!!" Aug 14.

Suddenly it was 'show' time in Malham. Remember, this is the township directly to the south of Malham Moor and has been inhabited since the 7th or 8th century CE, unlike the Moor where Mesolithic visitors "were probably coming to this district ... before 5,000 BCE." Raistrick, p 5. On arrival, "I was interested to see a British Pakistani family out on the moor. England had just beaten India at cricket, and I mentioned the match. 'How did we get on?' said the eldest male. 'England won just before lunch' I replied, and the guy did a jig. His wife, in a head scarf, looked to the skies as if to say 'what is he like?' and the 2 kids, dressed like all British kids, showed no interest at all. It turned out they were Londoners, coming to Malham on Show day quite by chance." Aug 28.

"The weather was gorgeous, typical early Autumn high pressure, being in the low 20s by midafternoon. As a consequence, thousands of happy faces wandered here there and everywhere. My phone camera buzzed incessantly such that I later found it difficult to know what to include in the diary. A farmer, explaining his prize-winning bull to a couple, was a joy to be part of but the magnificent animal was too shaded to be seen. As I'd seen the leaders run through the stream in one of the fell races, I went to see the start of the next in the show ground itself and got the pic below which, I think, really captures what show day means." Aug 28.

One of the younger age fell races starts from the show ground on a glorious afternoon.

"I finished the day by practising my limited Japanese with a young couple waiting for the bus to Skipton. The girl had been visiting the boy who is studying English in London. She said she was from Shizuoka and when I said "Fuji-san no ho" (where mount Fuji is) she seemed most impressed. She was returning to Japan in 2 days' time and I could not help but wonder how their relationship would progress and whether she would improve her English more than him due to her attitude. Lovely, lovely people and clearly very much in love."

SEPTEMBER

"Happily, we bask in this warm September sun." Henry David Thoreau.

Having found the quote above, I reminded myself more of who the naturalist, Thoreau was. I discovered he had also written about 'slavery', 'civil disobedience' and 'life without principle'. In the latter essay, he wrote, following attendance at a lecture, 'There was ... no truly central or centralizing thought in the lecture. I would have had him deal with his privatest experience, as the poet does.'

I have myself come to believe that the anxiety that humans appear to have, is the result of this lack of attention to this 'privatest experience' and one's own deep moral values. I had experienced this in my university work as more courses were focused on fitting in with the job market, rather than personal development and it was as though only about 10% of my Masters students wanted to engage with anything deeper than the 'starting salary'. Paul Simon's words about having one's 'books and poetry to protect me' would be quite lost on most it seemed.

This became pertinent when I noticed diary comments like this from Sep 8th: "Another very stressful time with threats to jab some of our teenagers. My eldest granddaughter has just gone to Manchester to study Finance and she's talking about threatening her childrearing chances by having a jab so she can go clubbing!" These complex thoughts can get you down when manacled to your computer, but, get out in the fresh air and all that changes. It may be that the outdoor, wild, environment is where true reflection, compassion and understanding can come from.

Arncliffe road, in shadow, bearing right from Malham Moor tops.

And the consistent theme of the lovely people one meets reminds you that these are the people you may have referred to as 'sheep' or 'bedwetters' and that there has to be a better, more human way forward. A great help is always Lee, mentioned earlier: "Lee has become my counsellor during recent times and his ability to listen and explain the 'other' view has become necessary. The mist cleared quickly and the chat with Lee was as cathartic as usual." Sep 15.

John Brown descends the last mile back to Darnbrook Farm

JB is a good one to practise on since we are very different but, hopefully, very human. The walk we did on 8th September, in an autumn heatwave, took us to the very northeast of the Moor. "As usual the route joined up places we had already been, starting at Darnbrook farm. We then headed along the quiet road until the PennineWay was crossed and we followed it to Malham Tarn Field Centre. Here we were supposed to find bottles of water but they'd gone and it was 27 degrees! We ate by the tarn before turning up the Monk's Road, somewhere we had not been since early January; certainly a different prospect today, and took the left track which takes you up to Middle House."

Later that day: "We then came to the wild, open ground on the west edge of Parson's Pulpit and several tracks led me to dig out the compass and check; just west of north then north. It worked and we were soon looking down to the farm with Darnbrook Fell behind. I was quite overcome, not in a weepy way, but just the thought that, at around 400 metres there was no-one around and never likely to be too many with the 3 Peaks/Pennine Way so close to hand. I got the shot above, which almost does it justice. Just a fabulous corner of Malham Moor."

One of the eastern connecting townships, Arncliffe, was the start of the next little adventure which led to an experience with another truly amazing person, Naomi. Having been totally fed up with myself: "I put a fly sheet up at Street Gate and then drove round and set off up the track at the back of the Falcon Inn. I was quite pleased with my progress but, eventually realised I was following animal tracks, straying too far into the open moor. Nonetheless, after much blundering, I found the right track, arriving at the tent just after dark. I had made little effort but found my meal deal intact and enjoyed that before drifting into my usual pattern of broken sleep."

Next morning, half crippled: "I stumbled 3km in thick mist to where the road turns right. Here I found a place to sit and a car stopped just past me. I staggered up to find what I thought was a young couple. It was however Will from the National Trust trying to put Naomi, a RN officer from Portsmouth, back on track. Will took us to my car and Naomi joined me looking at the atlas, finding her base, Catterick, to be not too far. I suggested I take her and she mumbled something about only having a credit card which I ignored. We turned up through Kettlewell and headed for Aysgarth with me spouting endless streams of meaningless drivel and she telling me about her life in the navy and her wanderings.

I realised I had a soul mate and that she must have pitched her tent not more than a mile or two from mine. Another coincidence had a card I had sent my parents from Portsmouth in 1960 above the radio in my car. My sister had found it and put it there and Naomi, 'my new soul mate', wrote her phone number opposite Nelson's boat! When she left the car and I drove off watching her waving, I felt most peculiar as though something supra-spiritual had happened. I felt asking for a picture to be intrusive, so I saved a space below and bless her, she sent me this selfie from the top of the cove:" Sep 16.

Naomi sitting above the long drop from Malham Cove to the River Aire.

OCTOBER

"Lovely October, your beauty compels my spirit to soar like a leaf caught in an autumn breeze."
Peggy Toney Horton

Beech trees in late autumn glory near Malham Tarn Field Centre (883672)

JB managed to join me for the first October trip (6th) on a glorious day and, after a quick visit to Kirkby Malham church, we were off on a jaunt over some fields, stiles and streams, purportedly going to Otterburn in the Malham township, well to the south of our normal area. Getting frustrated by the stiles, often with long drops, we cut our cloth and did a round trip stopping on a bench in Airton for our packed lunch. The second week, rather more showery, was also a church visiting day, with JB chatting to parishioners in Kirkby Malham and then berating the C of E at Elslack.

"Elslack church took some finding down narrow, sometimes closed, lanes. When we got there, JB couldn't get inside which got him off on one of his favourite topics 'why doesn't the CofE have a Marketing/Promotional team which keeps the places open and offers tea, scones and a bookshop?'" Oct 16. I concurred and we considered a plan then got sidetracked, as you do! Nonetheless, the interior of Kirkby Malham church, seen below, deserves a picture!

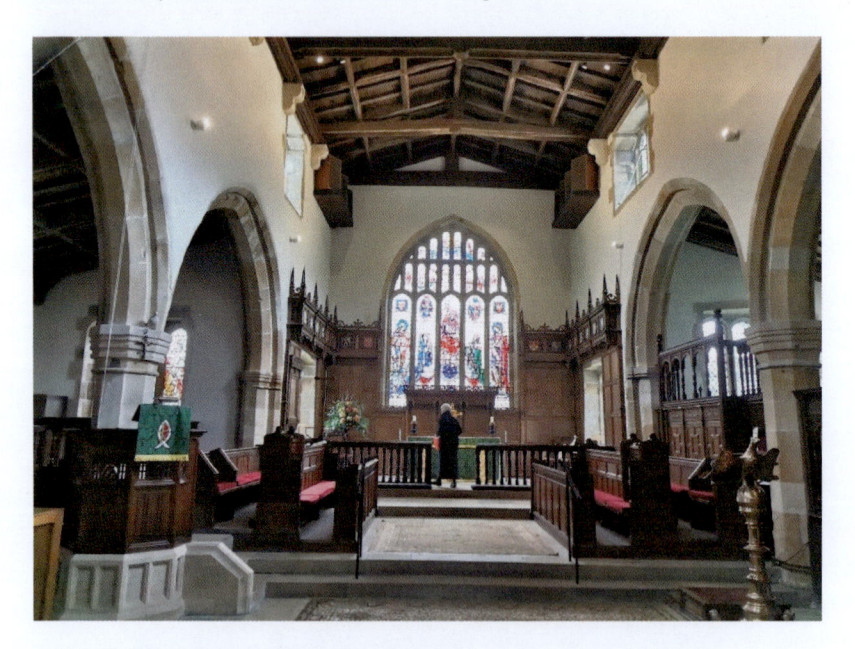

Inside Kirkby Malham church.

Surrounding the township of Malham Moor, going clockwise from Malham, we have Settle, Langcliffe, Stainforth, Halton Gill, Litton, Arncliffe then, to the south east, Bordley which even Yorkshire Dales fanatics can't find on a map. That's why it has a lot of charm and I've had a couple of runs up through Skirethorns to taste its special magnetism. On Oct 28 I wrote: "Drove up the lane, getting stuck behind a hay wagon. Doing 10 mph for 3 miles gives you time to ruminate and my thoughts were on the economics in front of me. Obviously, the load had been bought as winter fodder but how much does it cost and wouldn't the farmers at Heights Farm make more by opening a route round the caves, selling coffee and cake from a shack in the field?"

Hay delivery being stored for winter use

Thinking the same as JB had at Elslack, it's a pity we're too long in the tooth to start in Marketing! "Returning I had a fabulous sight of kestrels with the sun showing up their colours. Unfortunately, a lot of planning must go into getting pictures of these speedsters. I really must come one day to wait and see where they live and how they behave. It reminded me of Richard Leakey's word 'biophilia', **an innate and genetically determined affinity of human beings for the natural world."** Oct 28.

The picture below epitomises this side of the moor for me: "I came round the south side and found a road marked 'Bordley 4 miles. It took me up on to the moor, passing remote signs of the hidden nature of such mini valleys. The picture below of the bridge and its structure capture for me what it is all about." Oct 28. In fact, I went back to look for it to check the map reference but couldn't locate it!

Neat little bridge somewhere in the Bordley township.

I note when someone tells me how they love autumn, unlike Murasaki Shikibu in the Tale of Genji: 'You Autumn, I confess it: your wind at night-fall stabs deep into my heart'. Of course, being Japanese, that could be another way of saying how much he loved it! My final comment for October looks at the coming winter. "I was conscious of the arrival of the dark days. The darkest weeks are from about 5th November to the 5th February and, looking back, it is clear that early February really does have the first signs of Spring with flowers bursting through despite the snow on the tops. This gives me encouragement; just get through these weeks and a new dawn will begin!!!" Oct 28.

I finish October in the Lister Arms in Malham village and a reference to one of the world's greatest Sociologists, Erving Goffman. "Goffman had studied the roles people play working in a Shetland hotel and the theory of dramaturgy came from this. As Shakespeare had already said: 'All the world's a stage, and all the men and women merely players.' Goffman's theory showed how we learn our roles from other people and we lose our individuality through this process. Democracy and the inviolability of the individual argues against this." Oct 23. Pertinent in the time of 'Covid' perhaps?

My frequent visits over the years had got me to know many of the staff and some very nice, wholesome relationships have developed. As a result, you get to understand a little of the backroom roles that Goffman mentions, the personal stuff on top of the 'here's your coffee sir'. As a writer, having published about organisational culture, I have a great regard for the culture developed by the Thwaites group who own this hotel and a diary comment sums it up: "most creative organisations are those which can harness this individuality for group and organisational benefit". Oct 23.

Ross looks round to see a rare sight: JB opening his wallet. The moths are just out of frame!

The final word relates to JB who just keeps cropping up time and again; a most ubiquitous character, who I thank wholeheartedly for sharing so many trips and experiences with me during this funny year. So, there he is, in the above picture, with a little mickey being taken, just for balance!

NOVEMBER

"November arrived, cold as frozen iron; frosts and icy drafts biting hands and faces."   JK Rowling.

Up on the moor, just before the frosts, a young bullock fills his face along with his entourage.

The 'frozen iron' was to come later as the early part of the month was quiet and quite warm for November. On Malham Moor, it was actually the end of the month when the winter blast came in the shape of Storm Arwen! "Who would have known? In a survey of 100 people, Lee called me a hero and the other 99 called me a prat! "Thanks friend" said I and Lee replied "if people didn't try things, we would still be living in caves". And, what did I try? Well, having seen the prospect of overnight snow, I decided to go up in the evening, 26th November, and see if I could get a nice morning picture.

There was just one problem; I hadn't accounted for Storm Arwen! Mind you, it seems not many people had and at 8 pm everything was relatively calm and I drove round the moor wondering where to spend the night. I would have been better advised listening to the warning from Tam O' Shanter's wife, Kate: 'She tauld thee weel thou was a skellum, A bletherin, blusterin, drunken blellum; She prophesied, that, late or soon, Thou would be found deep drown'd in Doon;' (Rabbie Burns). The picture below is taken 12 hours later, encased in ice if not quite 'drown'd'.

Looking out of the car at first, icy, light. 8 am, Sat, 27th November.

As the evening and night progressed, piece by piece and inch by inch the weather worsened. Snow started slowly about 9 and then the wind rose quickly step by step; force 5 then 6 then 7; then it was Gale 8, Severe Gale 9, Storm 10 and Severe Storm 11. Did it reach Hurricane 12? I don't know but, in all my experience, never had I witnessed this and the later reports said there had been a gust of 98 mph nearby. I'm not sure quite when I decided bringing a summer sleeping bag was not the brightest idea but at least I'd got some sushi, several chocolate bars and, dare I confess it, a pack of cigars!

I think it was about every 2 hours that I woke and turned the engine on and the heat up to full blast. When it did actually lighten finally, I took the picture above from inside the car before a huge tractor pulled up and the driver shouted, "want a lift?" Did I want a lift? I was straight out of the car which was now encased like an iced fortress and into the pickup driven by Sue, the wife of the tractor driver Mark, and away we shot down the hill with me suddenly realising I'd left my phone on the passenger seat. No more pictures or communication for a while!

In the village Mark and Sue (Throup) changed vehicles and Mark took me to Skipton, having to turn back before Gargrave by a tree which had broken the walls both sides of the road barring progress. Mark explained that he had 6 trees down at the back of his farm (Low Trenhouse) and he had no electricity so couldn't milk the cows." Nov 27. I didn't dare tell them it was their son, Will, who pulled me out of a drift 10 years earlier prefaced in magnificent Dalesspeak by 'at what point is it t'brains kick in?' So I got a bus back home to Ilkley and went back 5 days later for the car. My great fortune was that Lee had got the picture below of the Lister as he arrived for work.

Lister Arms, 27-11-2021

So November came in like a lamb and went out like a raging beast. On 23 Nov, JB and I started late as "I was going to see the last part of Kevin Sinfield's run, 101 miles in 24 hours, for the Motor Neurone disease foundation. Sinfield, ex Leeds Rhinos captain, was running for team mate, number 7, Rob Burrow. I went to where the last mile was to start and encountered Lindsey Burrow and daughter, Macy. I explained that my 7 grandkids had all put in £7 since 7 is the number that her husband wore on his back in his legendary career. Seeing them and then Kevin, after 100 miles running inspired me and when I shouted 'Go on Kev', the ladies laughed and gave me the picture below.

Kevin Sinfield, Macy Burrow, Lindsey Burrow, entering Headingley.

My own health troubles went right out of the picture, particularly when I saw Rob's smiling face in the Headingley ground. The conduct of all these people was incredible especially in contrast to those who seem to just go along with everything the authorities tell them. As if Kev and Rob are not inspiration enough, it was the two quiet, unassuming, smiling women who affected me most. Absolutely A-star people, on a level of humanity way above the average!" Oct 23.

DECEMBER

"A winter's day, in a deep and dark December" Paul Simon

Despite Storm Arwen, the beasts survived, and the landscape went on just as it has for millions of years. "It was Wednesday the 1st when I took the minibus from Skipton and Debs ran me up to collect the car. We took jump leads just in case as it had been there 5 nights! Fortunately, it started straight away and I retrieved my phone. 2 days later, Friday 3rd, I was back with a mini plan of seeing what the damage was and what had blocked the roads." Dec 3. The scene below was repeated everywhere!

One of the victims of Storm Arwen.

Perhaps the trip of the month was Dec 18th when we were so lucky to have Slav join us again. Not only does he have a very youthful enthusiasm about him, but he also invited his '2 uncles John' to share a traditional Polish Christmas lunch on the 24th. My diary says: "I could just take solace from the fact that it is only 3 days to the Solstice, when the sun stops its march south and ..... stops! That's it; it stops and nothing much will happen for a week or two until one fine day a glimmer of extra light will show through and that will herald the end of winter and the prospect of tiny buds of colour.

Travelling through receding drizzle someone said 'It'll be warm sunshine in 90 minutes'. The other two gave him a weird look. Nonetheless, climbing the Cove road, we realised it was getting brighter and brighter and up top it was wall to wall sun! JB, as usual very keen to learn, was told what I could remember about 'temperature inversions' with winter high pressure forcing cold air down and warm air up, reversing the normal gradient. This is why the lowest temperature recorded in Britain, -27.2, was in the village of Braemar, contrasting with the lowest of -14.6 at the summit of Cairn Gorm."

Struggling, as had now become common, I decided to let the boys go off on their own and arranged to meet them later. This allowed a little more time for reflection which seems to come naturally when the days slow at this time of year. Ray Mears puts it like this: "the long evenings enable you to look back and contemplate the year that has been". This is particularly important for me as I ponder how to draw the year together in a final chapter at the end of this diary. I headed off round the Tarn.

Classic 'Temperature Inversion'. Malham village below, both in height & temperature.

"I had just passed several in a group carrying huge plastic covered maps, gaiters and ski poles in the bags on their backs. Seething at this amateurism, pathetic I know, I then spotted a youngish couple in wellie boots and pretty normal clothing. "Good for you" I shouted and they laughed when I told them my rationale. They just had an air of freedom about them and so I got talking. I found out they had started in the village in thick mist and had done the standard route up Watlowes, breaking through the mist at about 300 metres. One had no doubt chosen the route while the other probably followed wondering what was going on but, once they had broken into the warm sunshine, enjoyment levels must have surely rocketed; a day they will not forget." Dec 18.

As the year came to a close: "I was becoming more and more sure that my ailments were not going to settle and the thought of 'limited time' kept coming into my head. In other moments, I decided that moping would not bring any benefit, so action was required. The Malham min-bus driver had told me there were jobs available, so I decided to investigate. I rang north Yorkshire CC to be told there would be jobs advertised and also had this crazy idea that I might finish my Ed. D. so I searched for my old tutor, ending up finding another colleague who got a short email from me out of the blue."

The optimistic, let's get planning mood, was endorsed by some familiar feathered friends, the rooks: "On the way in the back door of the Lister Arms, I couldn't help having my eyes and ears drawn to the skies and, lo and behold, rooks were building their nests! Corvus frugilegus, having checked its Latin name, I found that it only lives 6 years which amazed me. Still, if they can communicate so cheerily, what have I got to moan about having had nearly 75 wondrous ones already?"

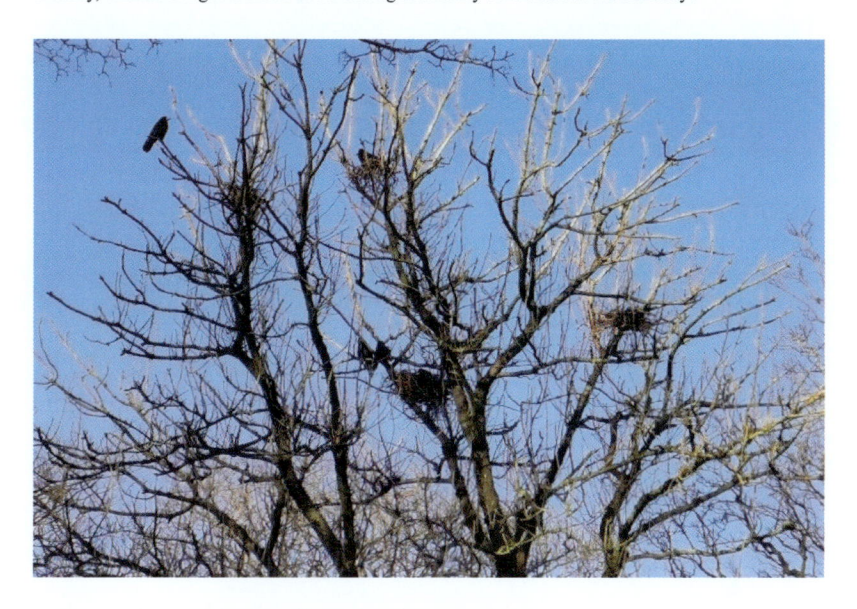

Rooks making their early New Year Resolutions

FINAL COMMENT

Redleft; Blueright.

In conclusion, maybe I love this moor so much because it is the physical embodiment of me and my personality. The gloves were an accident but fortuitous in a way because I think all British people, maybe all people, have a bit of Conservative and a bit of Socialist in them, topped up with a dollop of Liberalism and the more 'engagements' you have, the more you realise that the differences are not usually fundamental, just a matter of degree.

Understanding people became even more critical this year with many families not speaking as freely with each other as before. A great help came from Prof Mattias Desmet whose 'Mass Formation' theory says that most people were already suffering from 'free-floating anxiety'. They felt anxious but, having no lion or snake in front of them, deprived them of a focus. They were desperately in need of a focus with an enemy and a leader, just as other groups in history had been. He mentions 1930s Germany, the former Soviet Union, 'witch-burning' Swiss villages and Cambodia under Pol Pot.

The virus gave a focus and 30% went for it, 30% were sceptical and 40% just went along. The first group saw 'mask wearing' as a sign of regard for others so formed a group of, clearly visible, like-minded members. They are not interested in rational arguments. They have formed a 'mass' and they feel they belong. The latter group saw it as theatre with the mask-wearing a sign of submission to a totalitarian existence. Understanding this has helped me understand the other two groups and understand why they don't understand me. The real trouble is a fourth group of 'bad actors'.

This takes me to a reflection of Mahler's 'Mankind' theme and, looking back through the above chapters, what I am happy about is my obvious regard for other people, especially when I get close up. It is easy for a cyclist to remonstrate and dislike a motorist they have never met but put them together over a coffee and they find they have a lot in common. The work I did, with great colleagues Mike Spence & Guy Laughton, is mentioned above and we were ably assisted by the then director of the Malham Tarn Field Centre, Kingsley Iball. The key messages were the absolute importance of communication in small groups (teams) which are the heart of all organisations, societies and cultures.

While our courses, mainly for financial managers from the former Soviet Union, were run at the Tarn, the picture above shows members of the Leeds Rhinos 2022 squad having a 'bonding' day at the Lister Arms in Malham village. Having such a venue of comfort situated in such starkly beautiful surroundings provides a massive opportunity for these venues to offer exceptional opportunities for the development of strong, respectful cultures.

The very first words of Richard Dawkins 'The Selfish Gene' are "Intelligent life on a planet comes of age when it first works out the reason for its own existence" and this it may be argued, is the reason for such 'bonding' experiences as they allow people to come together and appreciate the value of listening to, respecting and co-operating with the 'other'. Whereas our managers were both male and female from Slavic and other cultures, the above picture shows the first 5, left to right, although all male, to be from Papua New Guinea, New Zealand, Poland, Nigeria and Leeds!

"Living organisms had existed on earth without ever knowing why for three thousand million years before the truth finally dawned on one of them", continues Dawkins, and indeed it is this self-consciousness between humans, in teams, which can help us to realise intellectually how co-operation can bring us together, provide huge joy and help solve the problems of those people and creatures less able to fend for themselves! It is this rational self-consciousness that marks us out as human.

Apart from the wonderful humans met, another of Mahler's themes is 'flowers' but, looking back, I don't make too much focus of this theme, probably because, when you are on the Moor, the flora is always just there forming a delightful backdrop. A classic comment of that nature comes from Jul 23rd: "something wonderful happened – the heat had mellowed, a breeze was up, and I was in a place no-one comes, not even the King of Malham Moor. I just pottered and enjoyed the air and the stupendous untouched wild meadow flowers."

Of course, 'flowers' probably means all flora in Mahler's eyes and some of the biggest contrasts in the previous chapters have come from the carpet of snowdrops in March, then the beautiful thistles in July, the golden beech leaves of October and the stark bare branches of December. Overlying all of this is the general darkness of winter and early spring, the greenness of late spring and summer and then the autumnal colours as the chlorophyll in the leaves begins to diminish.

Animals get much more of a mention, with a couple of pictures containing cows, bullocks, sheep and lambs and mention also being made of the extinct, former members of the Moor. As for birds, particular mention was given to the reed bunting, sand martin and peregrine but the kestrels must also be mentioned as they pop up regularly and are always a delight. Even the much-maligned Corvidae give us some interesting activity if we watch long enough: rook, carrion crow, jackdaw and magpie.

As for the mammals, Storm Arwen gave me some added respect to the enormous amount I already had for our bovine and ovine cousins. They all presumably huddled together in the leeside of the walls while poor humans dived under duvets in centrally heated dwellings. The term 'sheep' is one that has been applied by one side of the 'covid' barricade to the other but perhaps if people came and recorded how they live, a new assessment might be forthcoming. Quite the hardiest creatures I know.

Mahler's fourth theme was 'angels' and mention is made of my two youngest granddaughters in the April chapter. People often talk about the wonder of grandchildren as being the fact that you can give them back when you get fed up. My feeling is that that is a minor benefit, their beauty comes from the fact that they are, as yet, unsullied by the corrupt culture that surrounds them. I have four older than these two and all of them have given me wondrous moments when they were young because they were being themselves. Personality is everything and must be 'drawn out' by good teachers.

Paulo Freire says that bad education has a narrative which: "turns students into ... 'receptacles' to be filled by the teacher. The more completely she fills the receptacles, the better a teacher she is. The more meekly the receptacles allow themselves to be filled, the better the students are". Freire, decrying this "banking concept of education" says true "knowledge emerges only through invention and re-invention, through the restless, impatient, continuing, hopeful inquiry humans pursue in the world, with the world and with each other". Whatever Mahler meant, this is what my angels have and the release of kids into this wild moor has been a constant theme throughout this writing.

This little piece finishes with Mahler's last theme, Love, and it's clear he meant love of the first four themes. I share that with Gustav and hope that, within these pages I have also shown my love for the other themes which are the absolute treasures of life. In fact, for me, Malham Moor represents life and I love it!!!

Finally, little Luca (grandchild no: 7), with mum Luisella, on his first visit to the Moor. March 2022.